{DRESSED *for* THRILLS}

DRESSED for THRILLS

BY PHYLLIS GALEMBO

HARRY N. ABRAMS INC., PUBLISHERS

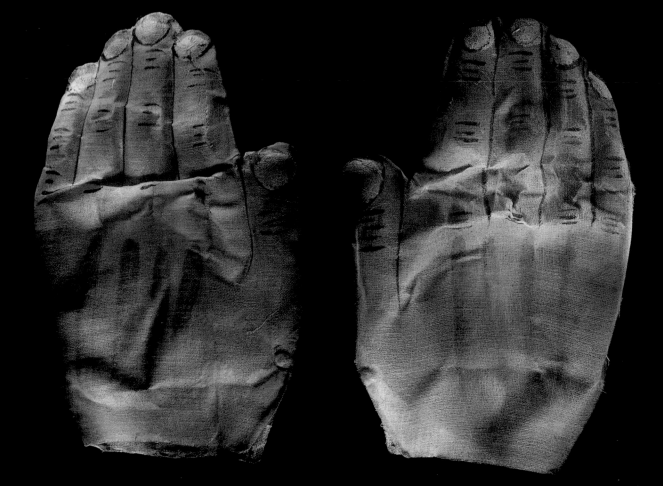

100 years of halloween costumes & masquerade

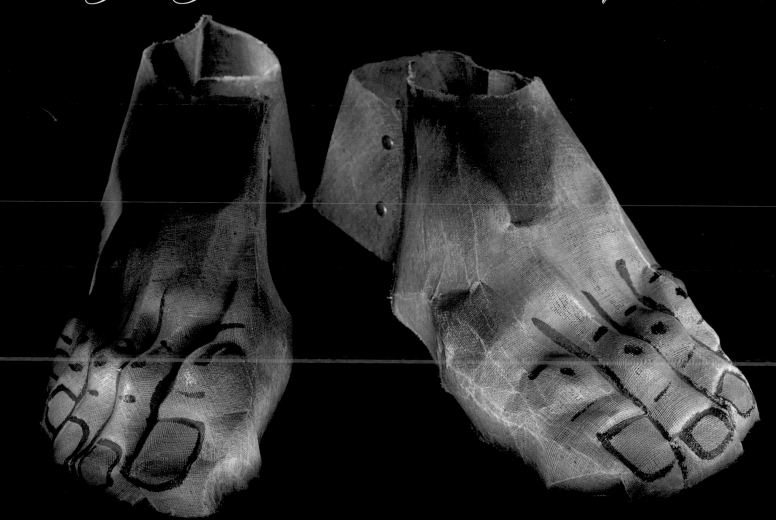

WISE WITCH c. 1940s, painted buckram mask, rayon hat. Manufacturer unknown.

(Captions for images on preceeding pages are listed on page 128).

{CONTENTS}

BONGO BEAR c. late 1930s–early 1940s, cotton flannel costume, buckram mask. Spotlite costume.
Manufactured by A.S. Fishbach, Inc., New York City, found in Marshall, Michigan.

DANCING BLACK CAT c. 1930, painted hooded cotton mask, cotton jumpsuit.
Manufactured by Yankiboy Play Clothes, found in upstate New York.

{P}hyllis Galembo's photographs of Halloween and masquerade costumes remind us that collective sartorial transformation is suggestive of alternative realities. In her previous works, *Divine Inspiration from Benin to Bathia* and *Vodou: Visions and Voices of Haiti*, Galembo explored rituals designed to facilitate communication with other worlds. Halloween also evokes the supernatural. Although most people today think of it primarily in terms of children's costumes, Halloween retains its symbolic role as the site of mutability. Not only are certain masks and costumes—such as those of witches, ghosts, and devils— overtly supernatural, but even the most innocent disguises enable their wearers to act out fantasies of transformation. To dress as a pirate, for example, is to escape from the constraints of ordinary life and adopt a new identity.

The subversive potential of masquerade has long been recognized. Writing in *The Spectator* in the early 1700s, Joseph Addison argued that masqueraders dressed as they "had a mind to be." To "masque the face" is "t'unmasque the mind," agreed Henry Fielding. Yet if masquerade costumes disguised one's true identity while covertly expressing hidden desires, much the same could be said of fashionable dress. As Fielding wrote in another context, the world is nothing but "a vast masquerade," where the majority "appear disguised under false Vizors and Habits."

Fashion has often been regarded with suspicion and disdain, in part because it functions as a mask rather than a mirror of the "true" inner self. Fashion is mutability itself, in contrast to the "eternal verities" of art. Yet, like photography, which notoriously "freezes time," fashion embodies the fleeting moment and makes visible the metamorphoses of the human psyche. With her extraordinary photographs of historic Halloween and masquerade costumes, Phyllis Galembo has made a significant contribution to our understanding of the power of fantasy in fashion . . . and in life.

valerie steele

Chief Curator and Acting Director,
The Museum at the Fashion Institute of Technology

MARIE c. 1920s, painted lightweight cardboard mask, wool hair, stiffened cotton rose.
Manufacturer unknown, found in Oregon City, Oregon.

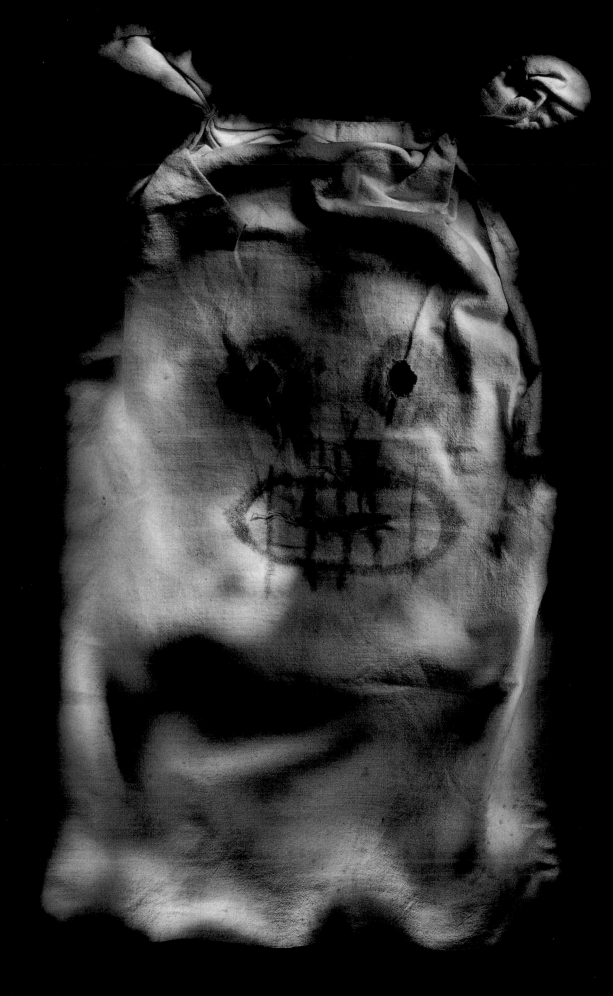

DEPRESSION-ERA GHOST MASK c. 1930s, ink on cotton pillowcase. Homemade.

GLOWING TURNIPS, POINTY BLACK HATS & INSOMNIAC ALIENS

THE HYBRID HISTORY OF HALLOWEEN *by mark alice durant*

For many of us the classic American Halloween evokes memories of cool blue nights lit by the flickering of ghoulish faces carved into pumpkins. A shivering excitement of mischief and expectant sweets filled us as we were tucked into homemade costumes of hoboes, princesses, vampires, and ghosts. Or perhaps our faces perspired behind TV-inspired molded plastic masks of Dick Tracy, Fred Flintstone, Wonder Woman, or Bart Simpson, while cardboard cutouts of black cats, gravestones, and witches decorated our windows. For some of us a hayride, getting toasty by a bonfire, and a visit to a "haunted house" cobbled together by a local community organization to raise money for charity were also part of our yearly autumnal festivities. Do you remember the taste of wintergreen on elaborately exaggerated wax lips? What most of us do not realize is that the cluster of activities that characterizes our notions of Halloween is a hybrid of ancient practices woven into contemporary trends in commercial culture. When we celebrate Halloween, we participate in that strange narrative we call history. On a long and circuitous path that begins in pre-Christian Europe, we find ourselves standing on strangers' doorsteps, shouting for candy from behind plastic masks.

Phyllis Galembo's photographs of antique and modern Halloween masks and costumes reveal many of the styles and variations that this ancient tradition has manifested in America over the last one hundred years. She approaches her subjects—pirates and astronauts, buck-toothed ghosts and long-nosed witches, dogs and pussycats, Cleopatra and Howdy Doody—whether store-bought or handmade, out of satin or polyester, with the delight and wonder of having discovered an entire cast of characters backstage of an old abandoned theater. In her capable hands they once again perform their little tricks, recite their sad soliloquies, and repeat their humble gestures of transformation. These painted masks, these ersatz gowns, these down-on-their-luck personages, whether recognizable or obscure, plug directly into our memories of childhood play.

Even without manufactured costumes, how simple it was when we were children to become someone or something else; put a colander on your head and, presto, you're a jester, an astronaut, or a fencing champion. Tie a pillowcase around your neck, grab a stick and a trash-can cover, and a Roman centurion stands erect. A little lipstick, Mom's huge high heels and glass "diamond" bracelet, and a starlet is born. Children are relatively free

of fixed notions of identity. For the blessed ones each day brings new opportunities to cross the boundaries that for adults have become unbridgeable. Armed with a kind of innocent subversion, the guileless sprites demonstrate no respect for the borders between boy and girl, human and animal, animate and inanimate. As adults, we observe, with wonder and perhaps a little horror, their total lack of loyalty to our petrified definitions of identity. We feel a bit mocked, shocked, amused, amazed, and even a little jealous. In the joyous abandon of children we recognize what true freedom really looks like. Perhaps the traditions of Halloween are kept alive in order for sober and mature citizens to retrieve a little of the magic of that privilege.

For many of us the details of our own Halloween memories chart a course through cultural notions of "age-appropriate" behavior. As toddlers and children, we traveled in tight little packs chaperoned by doting moms, lagging dads, or reluctant older siblings grumbling under their breath. We raced up each walkway or down each hall, jostling one another for the thrill of pressing the doorbell and being the first to shout "Trick or treat, smell my feet, give me something good to eat." We never tired of this, laughing and howling as the sweet booty rained down into our paper sacks or plastic jack-o'-lantern containers. Hoping for Snickers® bars, Milk Duds®, peanut butter cups, and M&M's®, we complained bitterly if we received candy corn or apples. Later at home, after the controlled carousing of the neighborhood, the entire contents of our bags would be spilled onto the kitchen table as we lasciviously ran our fingers through the fragrant loot like hysterical pirates.

As we grew older, allowed to run with friends and freed from the overseeing eyes of parents, our ideas of Halloween began to lean toward the mischievous. Dares and nervous laughter punctuated the night, eggs and toilet paper the standard ammunition of our pranks. Costumes became more improvisatory: a sister's tiara and a false beard, a father's hunting cap worn over an arrow through the skull, a refrigerator box painted with bloody dials signifying a computer run amok, a body wrapped in tinfoil and a single enormous bloodshot eye becoming an insomniac alien. Gathered conspiratorially in dark fields or school yards, boys and girls no longer required spin-the-bottle to steal less-than-chaste kisses. The rims of bottles were wiped free of germs as they passed from mouth to mouth, cheap alcohol burning adolescent throats. Some might remember piling as many bodies as possible into parents' cars and spending Halloween at the drive-in movie theater, watching a triple feature of "classics" such as *Night of the Living Dead, The Texas Chainsaw Massacre,* and *The Last House on the Left.* Youthful wildness was ragged and real, the taste of Halloween flavored with the forbidden.

On Halloween we collectively give a nod and a wink to mischief, and because it is a folk holiday sanctioned neither by the church nor the state, it functions outside everyday notions of civility. Although it has its roots in ancient Europe, emigration and the constantly evolving and heterogeneous nature of our culture have led to a distinctly American celebration. The specific dates may be lost in the murky past, but most folklorists agree that the holiday's origins began with the autumnal festival Samhain, the Celtic day of the dead. For centuries before the birth of Christ and the eventual conquest of their lands by the Romans, the fierce Celts inhabited the lands of northern France, Ireland, England, Scotland, and Wales. The Celts measured their days by the lunar calendar and divided the year into two seasons; the dying winter season began on Samhain and the life-giving season of summer began on Beltane, which fell on the full moon closest to May 1. The celebration of Samhain (roughly translated as "summer's end") fell on the full moon closest to November 1, after the harvest was complete and the animals were herded in from open grazing. As if to renew the strength of the waning sun, bonfires illuminated the hillsides. This yearly ritual acknowledged the shortening days and lengthening nights.

CHILDREN'S HOMEMADE COTTON DRESS, detail, c. 1930s–1940s, roller printed.

Samhain was the first day of the Celtic new year, and it was believed that the souls of those who had died the previous year were especially restless this night. A porous border between the living and the dead characterized this calendrical border between the old and the new year, between summer and winter. The veil that separated this world and the afterlife was so thin as to be transparent; the spirits of the dead communicated easily with those still warm with life. As with most ancient cultures, ancestor worship was an important tradition for the Celts, and Samhain the most sacred of festivals. Predictions for the future and divinations of all types were thought to be most accurate during this period. Rituals were performed to release souls temporarily inhabiting the bodies of lesser animals and those who wandered restlessly; not yet having found their way to the afterlife. Horses, cats, and criminals were set afire inside of wicker-and-thatch cages formed in the shape of fantastic animals. Led by Druids, or priests, villagers dressed in animal costumes and paraded to the edge of town, where food and drink would be left on the periphery in the hope that the offerings would satiate the restless spirits and thereby spare the villagers' homes otherworldly mischief.

When the Romans conquered the British Isles, they attempted to bring the raucous Celts under their domination. Through the back-and-forth of resistance and assimilation, the imported Roman culture began to mix and mutate with deeply ingrained Celtic beliefs. For example, the Romans celebrated their harvest festival on November 1, by honoring the goddess Pomona. Apples, nuts, and grapes were the symbols of love, harvest, and plenitude, and were the central foods in their celebrations. Through a process of acculturation, the Roman traditions merged with the Celtic, and apples and nuts began to be used for divination purposes in Samhain rituals. A "live and let live" policy was more or less in place between the Celts and the Romans, until Emperor Constantine declared Christianity the official religion of the empire and the third wave of influence was set in motion.

CLASSROOM PHOTOGRAPH taken on Halloween during the early 1950s.

Over the centuries, Christian authorities attempted both to tame and harness the power of the rituals of those they conquered. The holy days of All Saints and All Souls, November 1 and 2, respectively, were established not only to recognize the lives and memories of the dead, but also to Christianize the pagan traditions of Samhain. In practice, at least in Ireland, the pagan and the Christian lived side by side with the Samhain festivities that continued on the night of October 31. This night was known as *All Hallow's Eve,* a term that eventually contracted to our beloved word *Halloween.* No culture is pure; tradition may masquerade behind the mask of immutability, but history shows us that virtually every cultural practice is a hybrid affair. When it comes to habit, be it personal or collective, humans are both flexible and stubborn. We can shape rituals to fit the realities of the moment, but we are loath to give up things altogether, and paradoxically, the more force that is put on us to change our habits, the more resistant we become.

Imperial Christianity discovered this truth repeatedly as it incrementally encircled the globe in search of pagan faiths and traditions to overturn. In A.D. 610 Pope Boniface IV, for example, rededicated the Roman Pantheon, the architectural hub of pre-Christian Rome, as St. Mary and the Martyrs, suturing the pantheistic past to the monotheistic present. Later, in the eighth century, Pope Gregory III, in apparent frustration over the Celts' stubborn attachment to ancient gods, rituals, and practices, counseled his missionaries to consecrate and absorb their pagan traditions and holy sites into the Christian faith. If the heathens worshiped a tree, he decreed, then bless the tree in the name of Christ. During the Middle Ages, the practice of many ancient rites was declared heresy and the related symbols were demonized by church decree. It was during this period of suppression that All Hallow's Eve rituals became associated with Satan, who, according to church authorities, assembled his malevolent allies to mock the solemn festival of saints with their own unholy revelry. In effect the Christian church created its own cult of opposition. With Lucifer at the helm, these leagues of evil included pagan gods, any spirit associated with nature, holistic healers, Jews, nonsubmissive women, and generally any nonadherents to the church's particular version of patriarchal monotheism.

SKULL AND CROSSBONES PATCH,
detail from 1940s commercial pirate costume, block-printed, border with metal threads.

Despite the ongoing efforts to suppress them, symbolic vestiges of Celtic traditions such as bribing unsettled spirits with food were transformed in the medieval Christian church into the baking of "soul cakes." These pastries and breads baked by well-to-do families were offered to the poor on All Saints and All Souls Days in exchange for prayers for their deceased loved ones. This custom eventually encouraged young men from poor households to visit the homes of the prosperous, offering songs and prayers in the hopes of receiving food, money, or alcoholic beverages. In many Catholic communities on All Saint's Day, the church displayed its collection of relics and paraded them through the village, accompanied by a procession of villagers dressed as patron saints, angels, and demons.

Yet another European tradition that has filtered down through the centuries, adding flavor to the American Halloween, is Guy Fawkes Day. Celebrated on November 5, it is

DEVIL BOY c. early 1890s, cotton jumpsuit with hand-embroidered pitchfork, hood with horns and cape, cotton knit stockings. Homemade, found in New York City.

PUMPKIN SCARECROWS c. 1930s, yellow cotton jumpsuit (left) with black cotton appliquéd jack-o'-lantern and black button eyes, red cotton jumpsuit (right) with stenciled pumpkin fabric. Manufacturer unknown.

PAPER CUTOUT c. 1910s, hand-stitched onto cotton dress. Hallowe'en Silhouettes manufactured by Beistie USA.

symbolic of the historical struggle between Catholicism and Protestantism in the British Isles. Guy Fawkes was a Roman Catholic accused of attempting to blow up the Parliament building in 1605. After his trial and execution, which was a gruesome affair involving hanging and dismemberment, November 5 became a national holiday of triumph, the eve of which was (and still is) known as Mischief Night and marked by fireworks, pranks, and the burning of effigies. "A Penny for the Guy" is the traditional begging phrase used by British youth in raising money for Guy Fawkes Day activities and is an early precedent for trick or treating. In Great Britain the spirit of this anarchic and violent celebration has spilled over into Halloween, and English settlers in America brought these cultural practices with them.

It was common for colonial Americans, especially in rural areas, to gather for harvest festivals, which, like the Celtic Samhain, were a ritual acknowledgment of the end of the bountiful summer. On the cusp of darkness in the dying light of autumn, the sweet fragrance of baking apples and roasting nuts filled homes as townsfolk ate, danced, sang, and gossiped before the long isolating winter set in. Community elders whispered tales of ghosts and goblins as the children huddled by the hearth fire. At a time when sudden death through illness, accident, or violence was far more common than a life long lived, ghost stories did not function as mere entertainment but built a narrative bridge between the living and the dead. Tales of hauntings and unexplained presences also allowed the collective unconscious to manifest its fears, desires, and questions about the afterlife in the form of stories and legends.

At these harvest festivals, through an odd assortment of games of divination, young women attempted to determine the identity of future husbands. Apples would be pared in a single strip and thrown over the shoulder, the apple skin falling to the ground in the shape of the initial of the young woman's soon-to-be betrothed's name. After having their hands tied behind their backs, maidens would plunge their heads into a barrel of water filled with apples in the competition to determine which of the young women would marry first. For the future husbands the harvest festival provided a one-night-only free pass for mischief. Outside in the frosty evening, under the cover of early darkness, young men released devilish energy by playing pranks on neighbors. Perhaps signifying the holiday's origins as a marking of the line between life and death, most of these pranks were "threshold tricks." Assaults on fences, gates, windows, and doorways were the most common. Doors were nailed shut, windows broken, gates taken off hinges, and fences de-picketed. These "ruffians" understood that this was a night of a different order. At a time of year when the light was fading and the cold was threatening, the line between the sacred and the profane, between abundance and scarcity, between the material and the ghostly, between the pagan and the Christian had blurred.

The formation of Halloween as we know it today took hold in America after the first of the major waves of Irish immigration in the mid-nineteenth century. Fleeing the potato famine and political and economic persecution at the hands of the English, more than one million Irish citizens crowded into the tenements of eastern cities by the end of the century. Naturally, the Irish immigrants honored the Catholic holy days of All Saints and All Souls, but they had not fully abandoned the more ancient rites of Samhain. Folk traditions, such as masquerade parades, found fertile ground in urban and rural areas as the Irish, along with many other immigrants, moved west. The carving of pumpkins, for instance, is rooted in the Irish habit of hollowing out turnips and endowing them with patterns and expressive faces. Lit from within by a candle or a lump of coal, these turnips were used as lanterns during Samhain–All Souls processions. The term *jack-o'-lantern* is attributed to the Irish legend of Jack, a man so villainous that when he died, he was rejected by both heaven and hell. Poor Jack's soul was condemned to roam the countryside with nothing but a glowing turnip to guide his wandering in the darkness. In America the pumpkin provided a more dramatic and expansive field on which to carve ghoulish countenances.

In addition to the successive waves of immigrants, the second half of the nineteenth century brought rapid urbanization and dramatic advances in science and technology. These forces were reshaping and reinventing America. Victorian culture from the late nineteenth through the early twentieth centuries did its best to absorb these changes while attempting to soften the violent urgency of these radical shifts. Middle-class Americans mimicked their English cousins as notions of etiquette, gentility, and domestic serenity became dominant cultural concerns. The wild spirit of Halloween did not escape the domesticating gaze of the Victorians, who sought to tame it with parlor games and polite parties. Long before the commercial manufacture and distribution of Halloween costumes, turn-of-the-century women's magazines printed instructions for making a variety of costumes at home. Games, treats, and

DONALD DUCK c. 1930, painted buckram mask, cotton hat, cotton short pants with five green feathers forming tail,

songs were printed alongside patterns. Thereby began the process of homogenizing the rough edges of Halloween's anarchic spirit. In the hands of the Victorians Halloween became an exercise in controlled excess, a quaint holiday for young people held in check by the velvet fist of gentility.

By the early twentieth century Halloween had been all but severed from its association with All Saints and All Souls Days and had largely been transformed into a secular celebration for children. Civic organizations took on the responsibility of organizing pageants, parades, and haunted houses, continuing the Victorian tradition of highly choreographed and controlled Halloween celebrations. What one cultural historian has called "masked ritual solicitation," the once-a-year socially acceptable threat of "trick or treat" is a relatively recent addition to the tradition. Although there is little reference to it before the 1940s, symbolically it seems to have multiple origins: the food gifts for restless Celtic spirits, soul cakes, and Guy Fawkes solicitations.

Commercial costume companies appeared in the 1930s. Attempting to appeal to a large demographic, the store-bought costumes represented a broad spectrum of characters; the ubiquitous witch and ghost were joined by popular culture figures such as Little Orphan Annie and Mickey Mouse. Before World War II, commercially fabricated costumes were generally made of cotton with masks of waxy gauze. In the 1950s companies such as Halco, Collegeville, Ben Cooper, and Rubies Costume began manufacturing the now-ubiquitous vacuum-formed plastic mask and the rayon costumes. Celebrities and characters from cartoons, sitcoms, and variety shows began to assert their dominance in the pantheon of Halloween gods. In the 1960s costumes of cultural figures such as John F. and Jacqueline Kennedy, the Beatles, and the Apollo astronauts were sold alongside an ever growing list of costumes inspired by famous and even obscure characters from now largely forgotten television shows such as *Land of the Giants* and *Beany and Cecil.*

For many "mature" adults Halloween has become a tame affair in which we chaperone our children or head indoors for masquerade parties where bad behavior is relegated to the

PIRATE PATTERN c. 1925, Pictorial Review pattern, The Pictorial Review Company, New York City.

dance floor. But in many American cities with large Mexican-American populations, the holiday has been revitalized by Día de los Muertos—Day of the Dead—celebrations. In Mexico, as in much of Central America, on the eve of All Souls Day people gather to participate in midnight processions and carry sugar skulls and special pastries to cemeteries to honor the dead. Like Halloween, Día de los Muertos is a hybrid festival that combines pre-Columbian Aztec rituals with Spanish Catholic traditions. Through cultural osmosis in San Francisco, as in most Mexican-American communities in the United States, the rituals and traditions of this day have become inextricably connected with Halloween. An alternately wild and somber Day of the Dead procession winds its way through the back streets and alleys of San Francisco's Mission District. Death is characterized by huge papier-mâché skeletons that flail at the night sky as hooded matrons cup candles in their hands while muttering prayers for the departed.

Just a few blocks away from the Mission District is San Francisco's Castro Street neighborhood, the capital of West Coast gay culture, where Halloween is a celebration of the very notion of masquerade and performance. In a carnival of visual impersonation, the Castro Street Halloween Parade displays, mimics, and satirizes every imaginable pop culture figure and motif. It is a night of explicit acknowledgment that what is "normal" is in fact a cultural construction and that most of life requires us to don a costume and a mask of some sort. Similar celebrations can be found on the streets of many American cities, especially in New York's Greenwich Village and New Orleans's French Quarter, where the boundaries between male and female, real life and fantasy are trampled beneath the stiletto heels of a thousand drag queens.

Halloween stands apart as one of the most complex, curious, and contradictory of holidays. It is a day that has persisted not because of state or religious recognition; it is a folk holiday, a tradition kept alive voluntarily throughout the centuries by popular demand. It has been argued that Halloween has been entirely domesticated, that its once volatile energy has been controlled, curtailed, and circumscribed by the prefabricated fantasies of commodity culture. Although there is more than enough evidence to back the claim, the fact that Halloween remains a thriving folk holiday speaks of our deep social need for a public celebration in which we are allowed to drop at least some of the constraints that rule our everyday lives. Whether it be trick-or-treating, an office costume party, a parade through a city street, a bonfire in a football field, or a barn-turned-haunted-house, Halloween allows us to publicly express our private obsessions and to view one another in the transforming light of flickering jack-o'-lanterns.

WITCH PRINT COSTUME c. 1920s, cotton dress roller-printed and decorated with pom-poms and bells, cotton hat lined with brown paper and decorated with acrylic pom-poms. Manufacturer unknown.

PUMPKINS AND BATS c. 1920s, roller-printed cotton with snaps and hook-and-eye closures in back. Homemade.

WITCH COSTUME c. late 1940s–early 1950s, painted buckram mask, cotton hat and costume. Manufacturer unknown.

SCARY WITCH c. 1930s, painted buckram mask, straw hair. Manufacturer unknown.

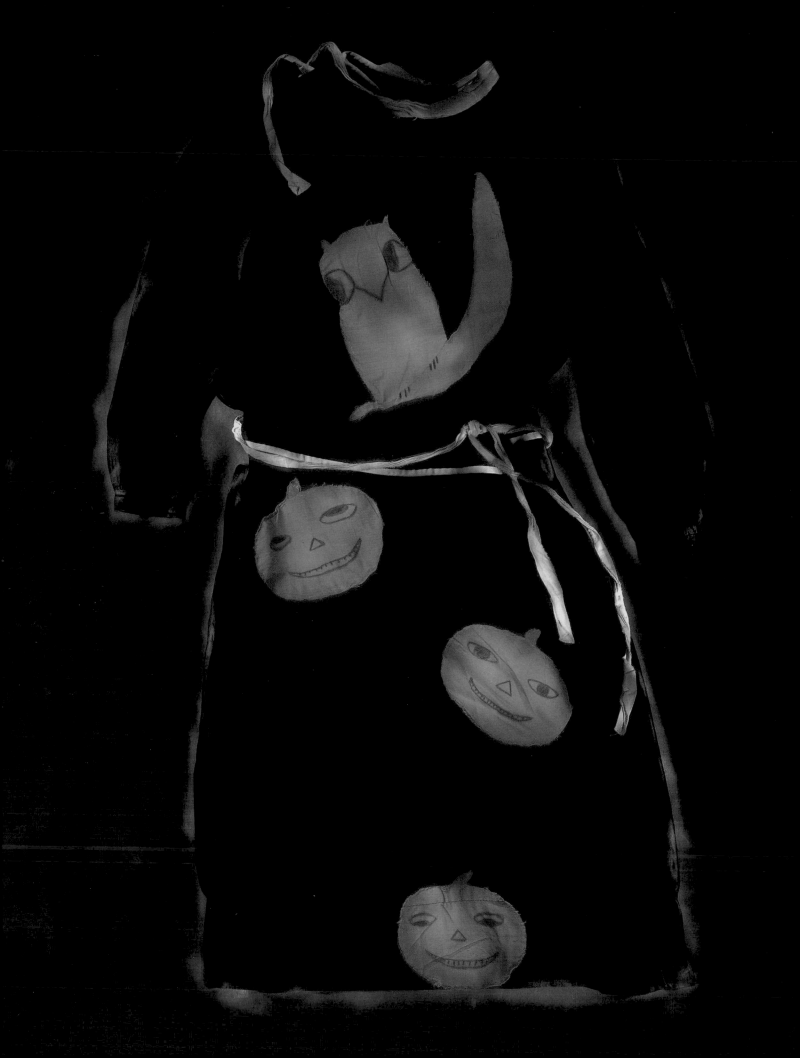

TWO PUMPKIN MASKS c. 1940s, painted buckram. Manufacturer unknown.

PUMPKIN OWL DRESS c. 1920s, colored-pencil-on-cotton appliquéd
homemade cotton dress with owl and pumpkins.

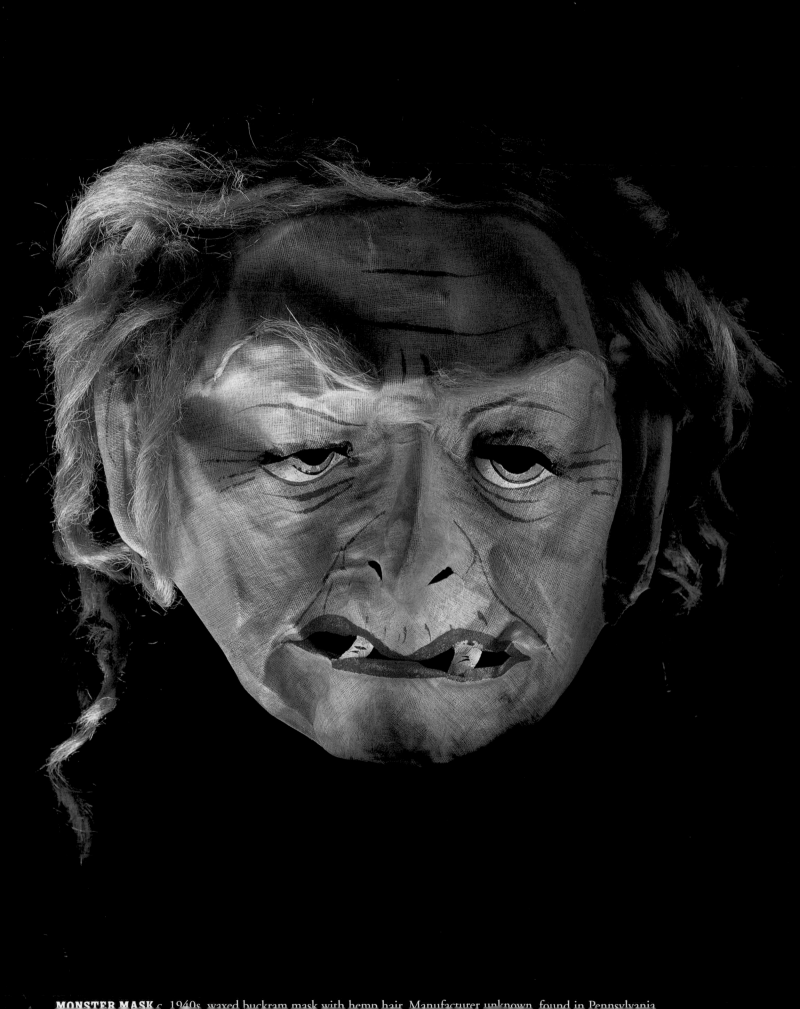

MONSTER MASK c. 1940s, waxed buckram mask with hemp hair. Manufacturer unknown, found in Pennsylvania.

{THE THEATER OF HALLOWEEN}

by mark alice durant

Each mask and costume pictured in this book can function as a kind of window through which to view cultural imagination. How are certain archetypes embodied? How do their representations change over time? What is considered frightening? Who or what is acceptable to make fun of? Let us not forget that the old Halloween standby—the witch—is itself a derogatory representation of women. As a handful of photographs in this book make clear, the image of the craggy old woman has become a satiric icon in Halloween lore (pages 30–31). The hag, the witch, and the crone were all derisive terms and images used to demean and debase the position of elder women, usually healers, who maintained positions of power in pre-Christian societies. With the arrival of Christianity, witches, or practitioners of Wicca, were forced to practice their healing arts in secret, often at night, away from village centers. Swarms of mosquitoes and big juicy moths hovered in the night air over the fires licking the bottoms of cauldrons. This vast food supply attracted hungry bats, which in turn attracted owls. In the eyes of devout Christians these nocturnal creatures joined black cats as animals in league with the powers of darkness. Today, two millennia later, witches, bats, black cats, and owls form an iconographic nuclear family forever associated with Halloween and paganism.

Surveying the growing diversity of twentieth-century characters represented in these images, we see that not only do the costumes reveal the imagery of long-held superstitions and obsessions, but by default or by design some costumes illustrate the explicit or expose the implicit social inequalities and prejudices that mark our more recent history as well. "Character wigs" such as the "Indian," "Negro," "Chinese," and "Irish" are an instructional index of cultural stereotypes that were commonly held at the time of their manufacture. The "Topsy" mask (p. 98) is a painful reminder of how Black children were mocked in the trickle-down racism of an America scarred by the legacy of slavery. Galembo has made a picture of this mask that, although it does not flinch from its objectionable origins, somehow brings to it new life. A miracle perhaps to be found in the fact that this mask, meant to demean African-American heritage, in so many ways resembles ritual masks of Africa. Galembo recognized this and, through the theatrical transformation of her photography, has reframed the mask so that it is reborn with a mysterious power that transcends its sad beginnings.

Galembo's photographs of masks alone are like visual non sequiturs; they initially promise the payoff of recognition but remain uncannily unfamiliar. For example, a handmade mask floats upon a magenta taffeta background (p. 13); is it supposed to represent a beautiful lady, a glamorous movie star, or maybe a New Orleans prostitute? A frayed rose is tucked into her fluffy wool hair; painted blue eyes are darkly outlined and half hidden beneath heavy lids. Her papier-mâché face is puckered, chipped, and folded in on itself; the smudged mouth suggests a surly and cynical response to the viewer's questioning gaze. The face, though disembodied, seems to be wholly independent, a discrete being with no need for torso and limbs. It appears to us as in a dream sequence from a corny old movie—all blurry, as if seen through the gauzy haze of sleep. Despite, or maybe even because of, its campiness it also conveys pathos and mystery.

Some of Galembo's most intriguing images feature handcrafted creations. Ghost masks made from pillowcases are classic, simple, and thrifty; and they hover in Galembo's frames like spilt milk (p. 14). Similar to the previous example is a mask that is in no need of a body for its ethereal effect. It is at once silly; with its ears sprouting like an improvised rabbit, it could hardly be considered spooky. Yet its hand-drawn face has a crude directness that lends the image a paradoxical authenticity. The dingy whiteness of the pillowcase seems to modulate in intensity as if it were struggling to retain its integrity against the darkness that envelops it. A similar funny-spooky image is the "Bat" (p. 2), in which the pillowcase is dyed black and adorned with descending fangs. It floats over a gravelly earth, and the deep cyan of the background seems to seep into the very fabric. In many of Galembo's photographs in this collection there is a peculiar quality to the light, as if the objects reflect and emanate simultaneously. This effect is partly achieved through the mixing of light sources, colored gels, and the virtuosic use of a light pen, which focuses a small beam of illumination. During a longish exposure—three minutes, for example—Galembo will, in effect, paint the object with light, creating a soft bathing glow of otherworldliness that softly defines the edges of the costumes against the background.

For sheer tacky enjoyment there is "Miss Eye-Full Tower" (opposite). The costume features a black lacy brassiere barely restraining the big-bosomed torso and a skirt silk-screened with an exploding Eiffel Tower, both topped by a vacuum-formed mask of a blonde with full red lips, red glasses, and an angled beret. With utter kitschy simplicity Galembo has constructed a background of cardboard, Christmas lights, and clusters

MISS EYE-FULL TOWER c. 1950s, plastic mask, polyester dress, rubber chest and glitter details.
Manufactured by Bland Charnas Co., New York.

TWEEDLEDEE AND TWEEDLEDUM c. 1960s, plastic masks with elastic bands, felt hats with acrylic pom-poms, cotton twill shorts with brass buttons, cotton knit shirts. Manufactured in France, found in New Jersey.

of tinsel representing fireworks. How Paris, or more specifically, Parisian women, came to be seen this way, one can only guess; but it must have its origins in legends of French bohemianism exaggerated through the stories of American GIs returning from Europe after World War II. As with all of the photographs in this book, nothing is "real" within the frame. It is artifice built upon artifice, individual play within the larger societal play. These images, individually and collectively, are a meeting place of fragments of cultural imagination and the photographer's vision.

As you might imagine, some photographs have quirky little background stories. For example, after purchasing the "Tweedledee and Tweedledum" (opposite) costumes on the internet, Galembo imagined a simple tableau with a couple of children sporting the matching outfits. As if on cue, the art gods responded by having the Rodriguez twins play hopscotch on Fifteenth Street just as Galembo was walking by on her way to her studio. After a quick chat with their mother it was agreed that Danielle and Nicole would appear in the photograph. For "Little Bo Peep" (p. 40) the lambs were borrowed from a farm near Albany. The photograph's backdrop is a lurid blue-pink sky with fluffy clouds that appear over the plastic green grass hillside. As the lambs scurried around the studio, Galembo added another job description to her resume: animal wrangler. After the photo shoot Bo Peep and friends were loaded back into the SUV and, with the sheep incessantly bleating across the George Washington Bridge, the entire entourage headed back upstate as the isle of Manhattan receded in the distance.

On a fundamental level, all photographs are stage sets, and Galembo is no stranger to theatricality in photography. As a photographer, she labors as the director, stage manager, lighting technician, and often the stylist and prop master as well. In two previous books of photographs, *Divine Inspiration* and *Vodou,* she has explored religion, ritual, and por-traiture in diverse corners of the world, from Nigeria and Brazil to the elaborate theater of Haiti's indigenous faith. Priests, priestesses, shrines, and altars fill her frames with color, mystery, and dignity. She has tracked how African spiritual traditions have shifted and adjusted to life in the New World and how, through the legacy of the slave trade, new religious forms were born in the Americas. Although she is a fine art photographer by training, her photographs have served many communities beyond the limited discourse of the art world. Anthropologists, ethnographers, students of comparative religion, those with a general interest in Afro-Caribbean culture, and of course the subjects themselves have found a devoted and sympathetic set of eyes behind her camera.

LITTLE BO PEEP c. 1960s, cotton costume with wood hoop in skirt. Manufactured by Ben Cooper.

The photographs in this book are elegant, funny, mysterious, and sometimes even a little scary. These images are not simple documents of costume types; this book does not provide an exhaustive collection or a sociological analysis. The costumes are the starting point of invention and photographic imagination. The primary challenge to the photographer is how to bring these inanimate objects to life. How to resuscitate them, rescue them from their dusty boxes so that they feel alive as images. Galembo answers this challenge with the sense of play and pageantry that inspires the urge to masquerade in the first place. Purchased at yard sales and secondhand stores over the last dozen years and most recently on the internet, Galembo has gathered this parade of costumes in her Chelsea studio in New York City. There they have patiently waited, in labeled boxes or draped on hangers, for their cue to perform in front of the camera. Backdrops are painted and repainted, branches are dragged in from upstate forests, two-by-fours are recycled from the street, hay bales and baby sheep are borrowed from farms, fragments and detritus are assembled and reassembled to transform her studio into a low-tech fantasyland.

This compendium of photographs is evidence of Phyllis Galembo's obsessions. As her previous projects prove, she is fascinated by the ritual use of bodies, objects, and spaces with which to communicate with other worlds. Every photograph by its very nature is a time capsule, and Galembo's photographs of Halloween costumes reveal to us what our public imaginations looked like ten, twenty, and ninety years ago. Because Halloween is fundamentally about communication with the dead, Galembo's reanimation of these costumes is doubly appropriate. She brings to life what may have remained rumpled and musty curiosities. In her elegant and playful frames the costumes rise from the dead to dance, play with fire, jump from behind bushes. Her images make us laugh and shiver and maybe even believe in ghosts. 🎃

BLUEBIRD c. 1952, crepe paper sewn onto cotton, rayon beak, light blue breastplate snapped on at shoulders. Homemade, found in Okemos, Michigan.

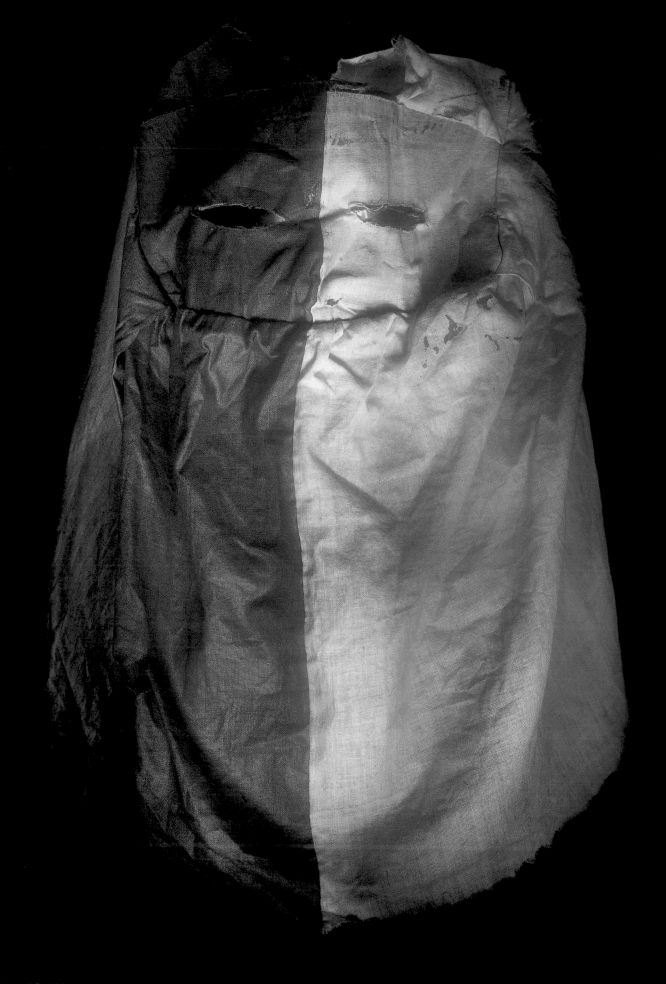

PIERROT MASK c. nineteenth century, hand-sewn cotton mask backed with stiffer fabric with pinked bottom edge. Homemade.

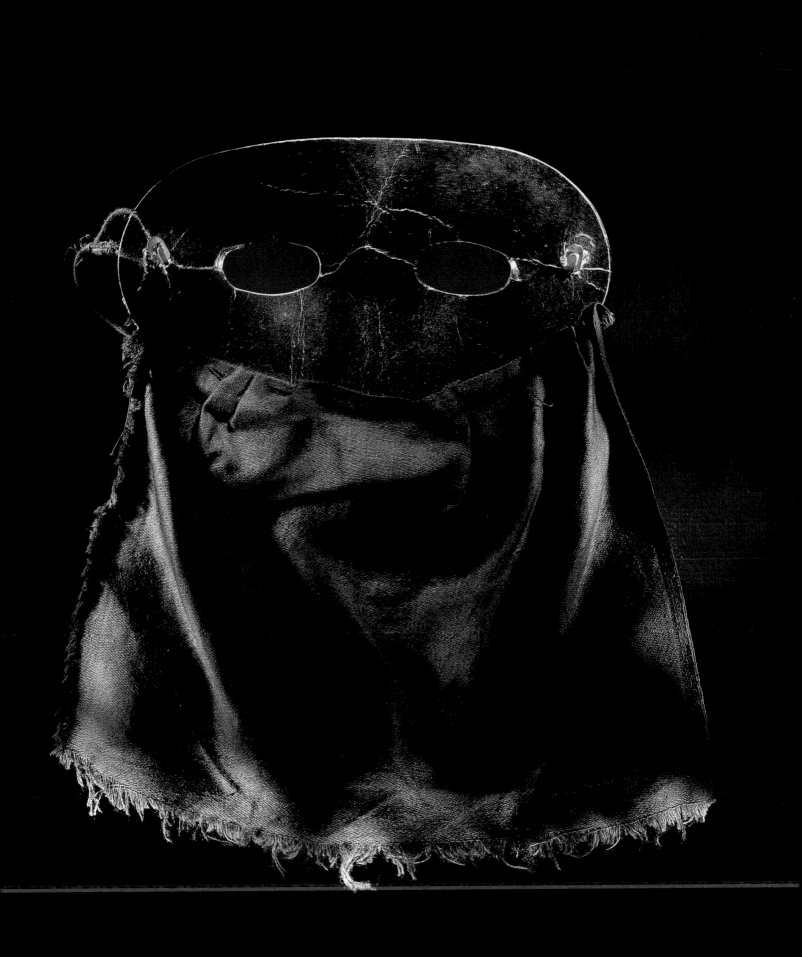

BLACK CURTAIN MASK c. late nineteenth century, cardboard mask with cotton fabric and elastic band. Manufacturer unknown.

DEVIL MASK c. 1950s, painted buckram mask with elastic band, cotton hood. Manufactured by Ben Cooper.

PINK POWDER c. 1910–1920, 3/4 cotton trimmed dress with gold ribbon, hand-painted cotton bag and leggings. Homemade, found in Massachusetts.

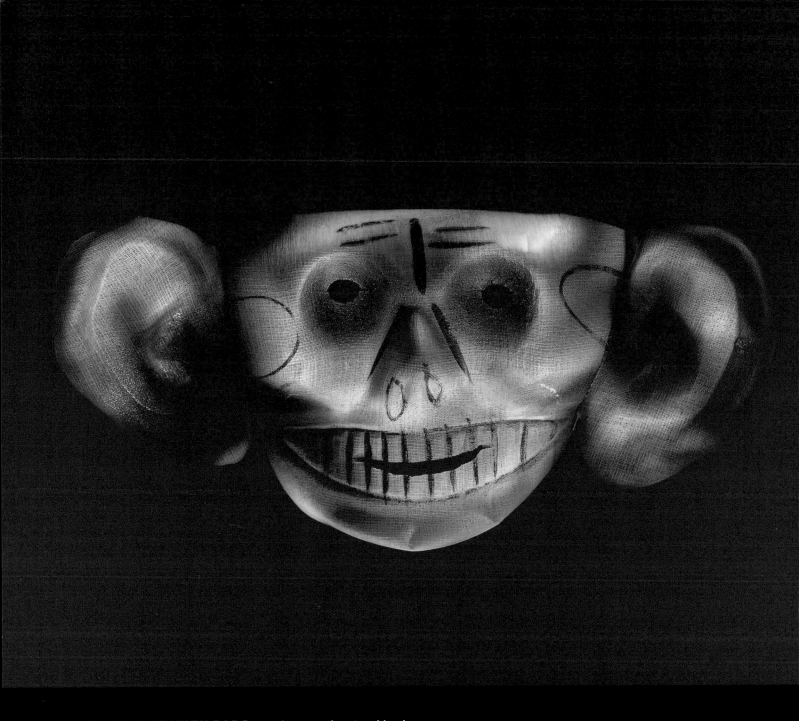

SKELETON MASK WITH EARS c. 1940s, waxed, painted buckram.
Manufacturer unknown, found in Pennsylvania.

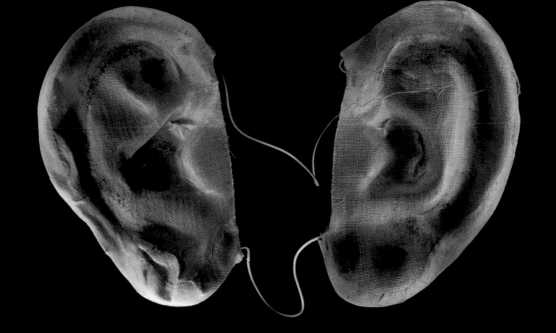

EARS c. 1930s, waxed, painted buckram ears connected by two elastic cords. Manufactured by Halco, found in Emporia, Kansas.

DELUXE DISGUISE KIT c. 1950s, all disguises rubber or plastic. Produced for FAO Schwarz, New York City.

UGLY FACE c. 1940s, painted and waxed buckram mask, crepe paper collar and bow, hemp hair. Manufacturer unknown.

by phyllis galembo

{As a child, Halloween for me was an important time and not a scary one in the least. In our home it was second only to Purim, the Jewish holiday during which children and adults dress as Queen Esther or Mordecai, important figures from Bible stories. To this day I remember the bric-a-brac on the dress that my mother made for my character of Queen Esther. I imagine this is where my lifelong obsession with costumes began and why Halloween to me has been more magical than trickster.

Beginning in the 1970s, the focus of my photography centered around photographing subjects wearing holiday or festival costumes. The ritual aspects of theatrical costumes in tableau settings also always interested me. My color photographs featured my friends as upside-down Easter baskets or driving cardboard cars or festooned in ribbons and American flags and numerous other regalia. This studio work held my interest for a long period but decidedly evolved following my 1985 travel to Nigeria to photograph traditional priests and priestesses and ceremonial shrine objects. After many years repeatedly photographing there and later in Brazil, I photographed the traditional priests and priestesses, and the initiates of Candomblé, the ancient African spiritual religion. Candomblé was brought to the New World during the Atlantic slave trade of the sixteenth century, and this specific religion with its riot of color and ceremony has always interested me. Through these experiences I began to understand the spiritual nature of clothing and its impact on both wearer and viewer.

I continued my interest in the spiritual and transforming power of ritual clothing and traveled to Haiti, beginning work on a new photographic project. My experience in Haiti reinforced my earliest connection and belief in the magical aspects of costume and ritual.

My interest in holiday clothing has now evolved into collecting Halloween masquerade costumes made in America. It began as a project for my four-year-old niece, Rachael, and her brother Robert. I had hoped to photograph them both in Halloween costumes I found in flea markets, on the internet, and in the outdoor market areas in my Chelsea neighborhood in New York City. Once started, I began collecting in earnest to visually illustrate my interest in how people use these costumes to assume different identities. At the same time I also collected props and ephemera for the tableau settings I intended to make. It was not my original intent to create a collection that would overflow my apartment, but it did! Shopping on the internet allowed me access to all of America and beyond—the boxes literally arrived daily during my

MIDNIGHT PRINCESS c. 1920s, cotton dress with glued-on paper stars. Homemade.
CROWN c. 1920s, thin wood band steamed into a circle and covered with black gauze and gold metallic thread. Homemade.

first year of shopping on-line. I was pleased that often I was the only one who appeared to have any interest in the saddest of costumes—a piece of cotton with a cork attached quickly became a dog with dignity and soul through the lens of my view camera (p. 106).

In 1998 I found a wonderful studio four blocks from my apartment while attending a vodou ceremony in Chelsea, so I considered it a blessing, if not an omen. I was destined to collect and preserve the made-in-America tradition of the Halloween costume. For the next four years I photographed more than two hundred of my five hundred costumes, creating a special setting for each and finding the perfect model for each as well. I've always felt I have good photo karma, finding the necessary props and especially the children to model, some-times by chance encounters on the streets of New York or, more often, the children of friends.

Many people have asked me how I decided on the costumes I was interested in pho-tographing. The earliest costumes I found, beginning with the late nineteenth century, were always of interest: People painted and sewed them by hand. This remained true up to the mid-twentieth century. The ones that began to appear in mass during the 1980s were mostly licensed and quite commercial, and rarely held my interest.

Working in my studio, constantly handling the numerous costumes, I began to feel the spirit and life each one held. I would lay a simple item, such as a dress, on colored board or a pile of fabric, or wire it up to float in space. After covering all my studio windows, I would hold a hand-built tool resembling a flashlight and gently "paint" with light around the object, bringing out all the details. Using a three- to five-minute exposure, my 4x5 view camera posed precariously on a tripod, I would find the soul of the object's past life. Depending on the subject, sometimes my hand movement would be slow and deliberate to provide a fine line or emphasis, such as causing Minnie's dress to glow (p. 62); other times I jerked my hand to create jagged forms, such as the outline of a skeleton (opposite). By using this subtle method of photographing, the items appeared to come alive—as though the soul of the last person who wore the item was appearing.

Bringing out the playful nature of the costume is a joy. A skeleton's green polyester hair becomes frighteningly intense when placed on a 1960s neon board (opposite). Frozen, dried-out banana leaves become transformed when three monkey masks of buckram (a gauzelike material) hover above the surface (p. 66).

Not all the costumes evoke humor. Isolated wigs, such as the "Negro" wig made of string, horsehair, and twine, give me pause when I think of the derogatory use such costumes would have had in the past (p. 57). It is hard to believe these costumes were ever acceptable. They even appeared in costume catalogs until the 1950s. Yet when the costumes are seen in numbers, you

HAIRY SKELETON c. 1965, plastic mask with nylon hair, elastic fastener. Manufactured by Collegeville Costumes, found in Crown Point, Indiana.

HEP CATS early 1950s, rayon jumpsuits, plastic masks (one with bells). Manufactured by Ben Cooper.

realize that many early Halloween costumes and traditions may have been influenced by black culture. The Jester mask (p. 99), for instance, reminds me of the Nigerian ancestral spirit Egúngún. On another costume (opposite), the words "Hep Cat" come from the Senegalese Wolof *hepe* (eyes open, to be aware) and *kat* (an aware person who knows what's happening).

To create all the settings I required, my studio was constantly in a state of transformation. At one point it turned into a marsh with the wild rice I had collected upstate, along with cattails and other ephemera and the use of multiple exposures. At another time there were the hobo's tracks (p. 120) and the mammy shack (p. 80); and the next week, Bo Peep (p. 40).

Homemade masquerade costumes appeared in the late 1800s and later gave way to active commercial production at the time of the Industrial Revolution, both of which continue to this day. The Dennison Manufacturing Company in Massachusetts began making paper costumes in 1910, and others joined in the production. Collegeville, located in Collegeville, Pennsylvania, began as a company that produced flags and later, around 1910, used the scraps to create early clown and jester costumes. The company continues to this day as Collegeville Imagineering. The Ben Cooper Company was founded by its namesake in 1927. Based in Brooklyn, New York, Cooper created theatrical sets and costumes for the Cotton Club and the Ziegfeld Follies, and expanded into Halloween costumes in 1937. The company later joined with A. S. Fishbach, a New York City–based costume company that held the license to Disney characters, such as Donald Duck, and packaged them under the name Spotlight. Cooper sold his company in the 1980s to Rubies Costume Company, also in New York, which has become one of the largest producers of Halloween and Purim costumes in the United States.

Many of the masks for the early costumes were produced by U.S. Mask Company in Woodhaven, New York. Their earliest gauze masks, made of buckram, were sprayed with starch and steamed over a mold. In the 1950s, vacuformed masks appeared. Other major costume companies in America included Halco, in Pennsylvania; Bland Charnas Co., on Long Island, New York; and E. Simons and Sons, in New Orleans, Louisiana.

In 1932 America participated in the celebration of the two-hundredth anniversary of the birth of George Washington. The U.S. George Washington Bicentennial Commission prepared booklets providing information regarding costumes that were acceptable for use in plays and costume balls. Eventually, many of these costumes were recycled to be used for Halloween and masquerade parties, and a few of the ones in my collection are part of this heritage (p. 78).

Halloween allows us to experience and explore the shared ethnic, cultural, and folk celebrations that have engaged diverse peoples throughout history. It is these common threads that inspire me to celebrate and document the use of costume and masquerade. 🦇

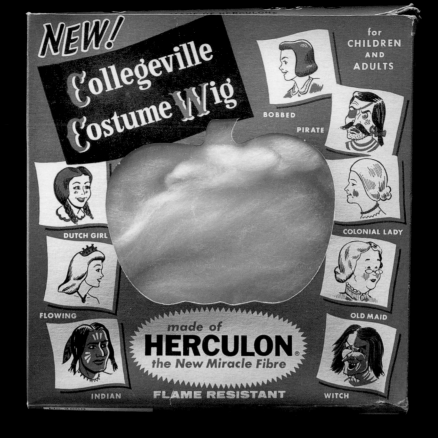

COLONIAL LADIES WIG BOX c. 1950s, originally sold at Woolworths for $.97.
Manufactured by Collegeville Costumes.

BLONDE WIG WITH BOW c. 1950s, rayon hair, printed cotton bow and hat pin. Manufacturer unknown.

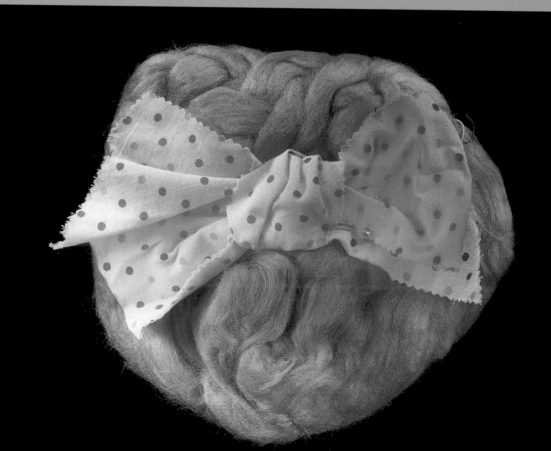

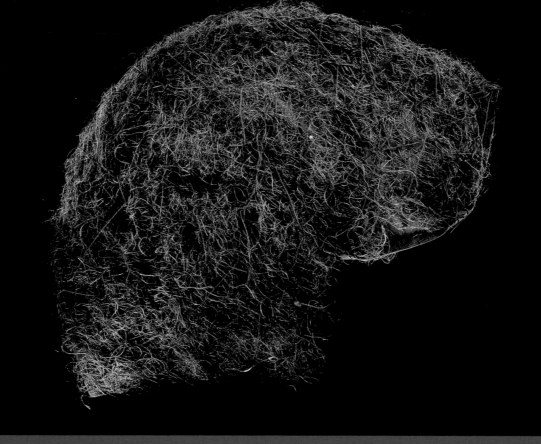

"NEGRO" WIG c. 1920s, horsehair secured to cotton fabric with heavy cotton threads. Manufacturer unknown, found in Georgetown, Ohio.

COLONIAL LADIES WIG c. 1940s, mohair with stiffened cotton flower. Manufacturer unknown.

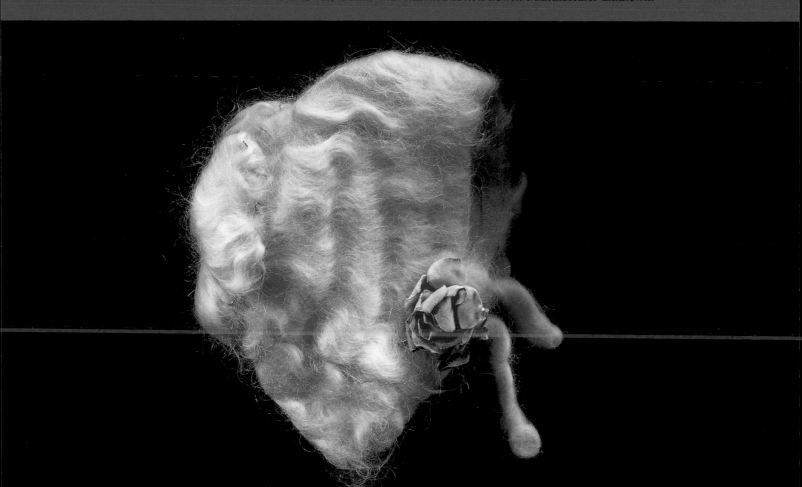

OLIVE OYL 1936, waxed, painted buckram mask with grosgrain ribbon tie, flannel shirt with snaps up back, flannel skirt, net wig with rayon hair and wide grosgrain ribbon. Manufacturer unknown, found in Michigan.

POPEYE 1954, painted rayon over buckram mask, rayon costume, buckram muscles with painted tattoos. Manufactured by Collegeville Costumes.

THREE FROGS c. 1940s, painted buckram mask with polished cotton back, polished cotton jumpsuits.
Manufactured by Halco, found in Oaklyn, New Jersey.

MINNIE c. 1930, cotton mask with gauze face, ribbed cotton-knit shirt with gauze circle on chest reading "Minnie," cotton-twill four-finger gloves, lace-trimmed cotton bloomers with elastic waist and ankles, cotton skirt. Manufacturer unknown.

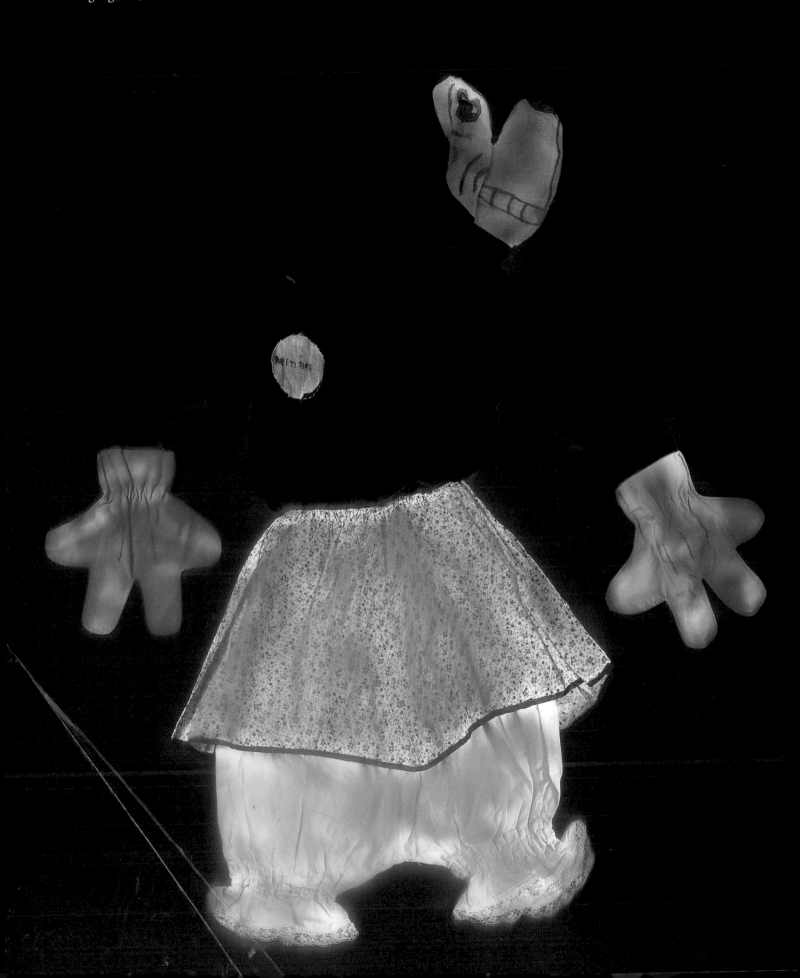

MICKEY c. 1930, cotton mask with gauze face, cotton shirt, and pants, cotton-twill four-finger gloves, cotton tail stiffened with wire. Manufacturer unknown, found in North Attleboro, Massachusetts.

RED RIDING HOOD c. 1941, cotton skirt with printed illustrations of Red Riding Hood story trimmed with gold ribbon, cotton cape. Manufactured by Collegeville Costumes, found in Lafayette, New Jersey.

BROWN BEAR c. 1940s, painted buckram mask with cotton jumpsuit. Manufacturer unknown.

PEASANT GIRL c. late 1940s, cotton-synthetic drawstring skirt trimmed with metallic ribbon, sheer nylon front and sleeves, synthetic vest and sash, printed cotton kerchief decorated with metallic ribbon and foil circles, rayon braids. Manufacturer unknown.

BIG BAD WOLF c. 1939, painted buckram mask, cotton shirt with buttons in back, cotton pants with elastic waist and buttons for suspenders, cotton-covered wire tail. Manufactured by A. S. Fishbach, Inc., New York City.

THREE MONKEYS c. 1940s, painted buckram masks with cotton-twill tape ties. Manufacturer unknown, found in Connecticut.

MUSTACHE MAN c. 1930s, painted, starched buckram mask, rayon hair. Manufacturer unknown.

WOMAN WITH HAT c. 1940s, painted, starched buckram mask and hat with polyester ribbon, rayon hair. Manufacturer unknown.

MALE ELEPHANT c. 1940s, painted, starched buckram. Manufacturer unknown.

FEMALE ELEPHANT c. 1940s, painted, starched buckram. Manufacturer unknown.

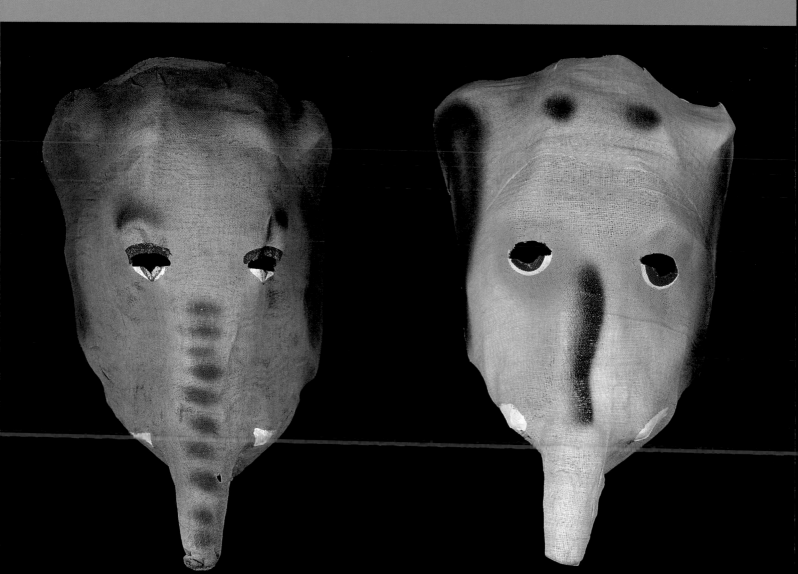

LIBERTY EAGLE COSTUME c. 1950, rayon hat with cardboard brim, painted buckram mask, cotton shirt and skirt. Manufactured by Spotlite Masquerade Costumes, found in Rochester, New York.

RAG DOLL c. 1940s, cotton mask with acrylic yarn, cotton dress and separate leggings.
Yankiboy Play Clothes manufactured by Sackman Brothers Co., Inc., New York City.

lined cotton trousers. Homemade, found in Pennsylvania.

LIBERTY GIRL c. 1890–1910, linen dress with gold paper stars, gathered waistline and shoulders.
Homemade, found in Pennsylvania.

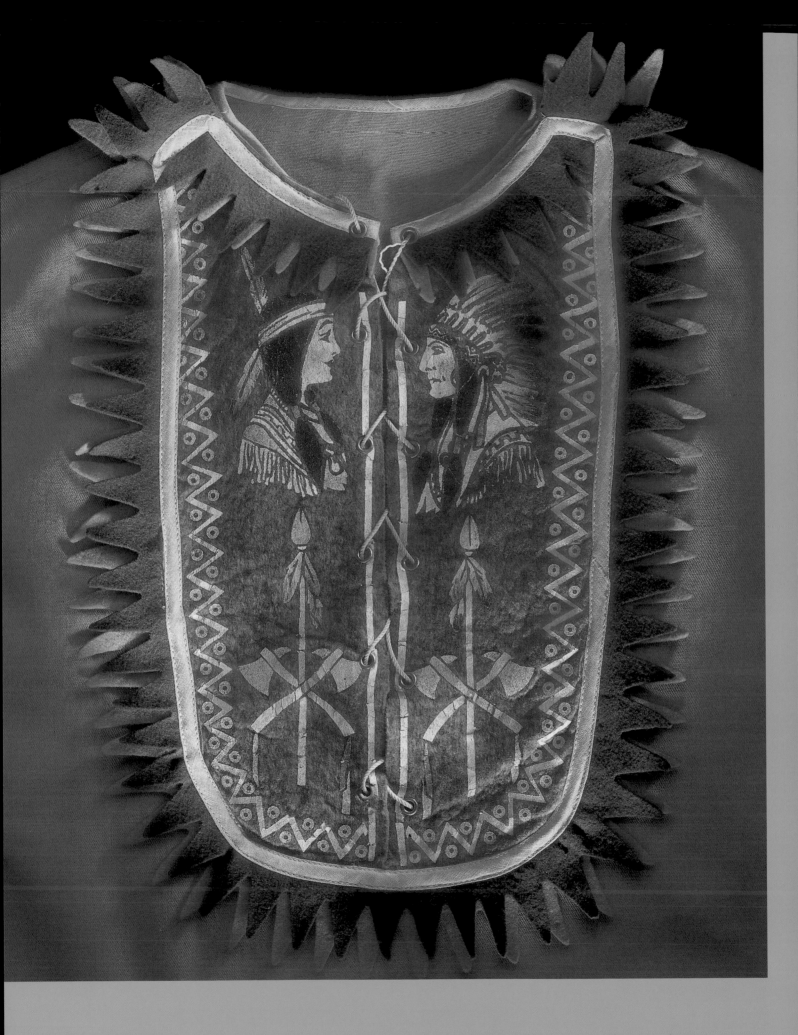

INDIAN COSTUME c. late 1940s–early 1950s, hand-painted design on cotton twill with felt detail. Manufacturer unknown.

INDIAN BOY c. early 1950s, cotton-twill pants with button fly and drawstring waist, shirt trimmed with felt; felt headdress trimmed with feathers, cotton strips, and bells. Manufacturer unknown.

left to right:

RIDIN'-N-ROPIN' COWGIRL c. late 1930s–early 1940s, chain stitch embroidered yellow blouse, faux buttons, cotton skirt and vest. Manufacturer unknown.

COWGIRL c. 1950s–1960s, cotton-flannel plaid top and tie collar, cotton leopard-print skirt, yellow plastic fringe. Manufacturer unknown.

COWBOY c. early 1960s, cotton-corduroy cowboy pants with faux red chaps decorated with lariat motif in colored ribbon with matching vest, plastic waistband laces in front. Manufacturer unknown.

COWBOY c. 1940s, fake pony skin chaps and vest decorated with metal disks and leather fringe. Manufacturer unknown.

BOLEROS c. 1940s, skirt, hat, vest, sash, and trousers made of napped acetate with cotton pom-poms. Homemade, found in New York City.

COLONIAL GIRL c. 1932, cotton velvet jacket, cotton breeches, trim, and side buttons, cotton vest, linen shirt.
Manufacturer unknown.

PILGRIM SHIRT c. 1930s–1940s, cotton shirt with lace jabot and foil-covered cardboard buckles. Homemade, found in Massachusetts.

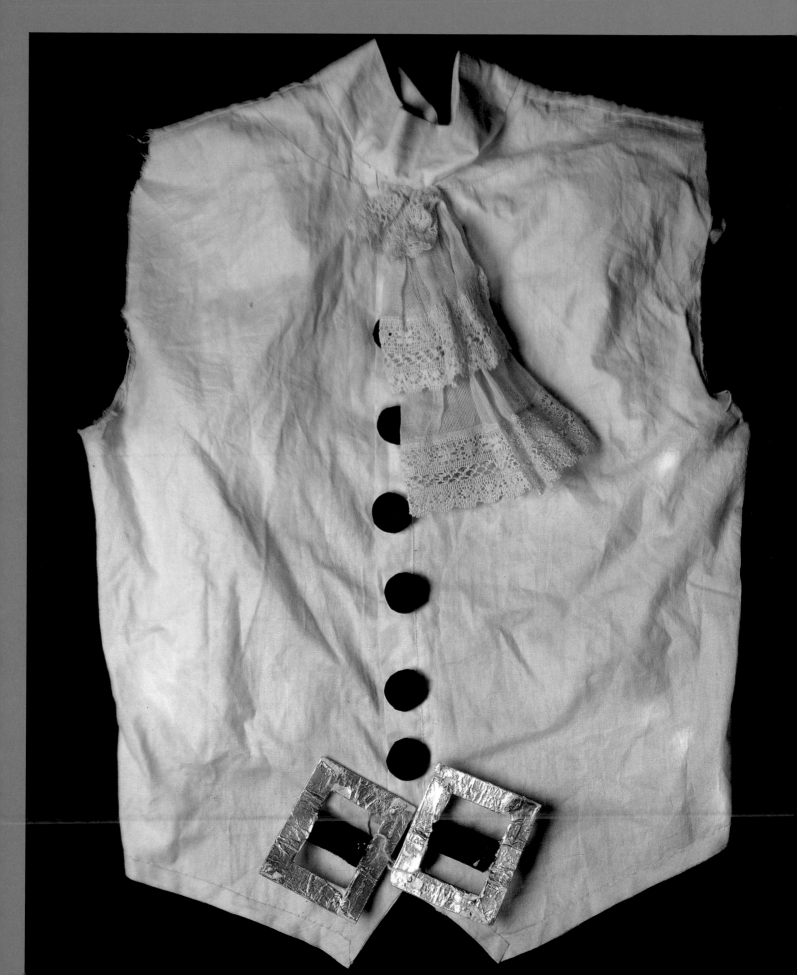

ASIAN PRINCESS c. 1958, plastic mask, rayon dress with gold glitter pagoda design on front and quasi-Asian characters around edges. Manufactured by Ben Cooper.

MAMMY c. 1915–1925, painted buckram mask, cotton kerchief, jumpsuit, slip, and apron. Manufacturer unknown, found in Loganville, Pennsylvania.

PILGRIM CHILD c. 1940s, cotton-polyester-blend costume, cotton-polyester blend hat over cardboard brim,

PUMPKIN BOY c. 1940s, cotton with appliquéd eyes, nose, and mouth, plus embroidered details. Homemade.

HARLEQUIN c. 1938, cotton jumpsuit and hat lined with New York City newspaper advertising the movie *Love Finds Andy Hardy*. Manufacturer unknown.

HARLEQUIN DRESS c. 1950s, rayon mask, cotton skirt and lightly boned top, rayon slip with gauze ruffles, cotton-over-cardboard hat lined with quilted satin. Manufacturer unknown, found on Long Island, New York.

DUTCH BOY c. 1940s, polished cotton costume, canvas hat. Manufacturer unknown, found in New Orleans.

CLEOPATRA c. 1960s, front side (left) manufactured, backside (right) with hand-appliquéd glitter and rubber snake. Manufacturer unknown, found in Hackettstown, New Jersey.

Text on costume:

CLEOPATRA PLAYSUIT

WHEN THERE'S "NOTHING TO WEAR"
I COMB DOWN MY HAIR,
JUT SLIP ON THIS STYLE
AND I'M QUEEN OF THE NILE.

POLKA-DOT DOG c. 1940, homemade cotton jumpsuit closed with three ties in back, commercially produced rubber mask. Mask manufacturer unknown, found in Spokane, Washington.

HOWDY DOODY c. 1950, painted rayon over buckram mask. Manufactured by Collegeville Costumes.

CLARABELLE THE CLOWN (from "Howdy Doody") c. 1950s, cotton jumpsuit. Manufactured by Bland Charnas Co., found in Platteville, Wisconsin.

CHARLIE MCCARTHY c. 1938, painted buckram mask with plastic lensless monocle and elastic fastener, cotton jacket and pants with drawstring waist, cotton top hat with wire brim. Manufactured by Collegeville Costumes, found in Beverly Hills, California.

LITTLE ORPHAN ANNIE c. 1936, waxed, painted buckram mask, cotton dress that snaps in back.
Manufactured by Collegeville Costumes, found in Williamsport, Pennsylvania.

LARGE CLOWN HEAD c. 1959, plastic mask, rayon costume. Manufactured by Halco, found in San Francisco, California.

CLOWN HAT c. 1920s–1930s, paper. Manufacturer unknown, made in Germany, found in New York City.

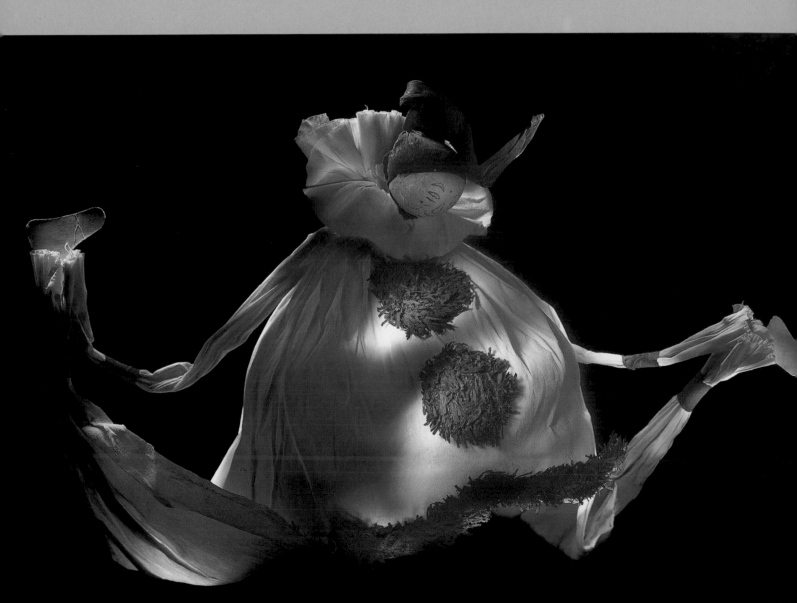

JESTER MASK c. 1910–1920, cotton fabric with "two-part bells." Homemade, found in New Hampshire.

PIERROT CHILD c. 1940s, cotton jumpsuit and hat. Manufacturer unknown, found in New York City.

JESTER c. 1895–1897, calendered cotton top, skirt, hat, and shoes. Homemade, found in Connecticut.

HEART DRESS c. 1920s–1930s, mask and cotton dress, with suspended cotton-covered cardboard hearts. Homemade, found in Lynchburg, Virginia.

CHRISTMAS DRESS c. 1890s, polished cotton dress (with detail) and some twentieth-century ornaments added later. Homemade, found in Massachusetts.

PETER COTTONTAIL c. late 1950s, painted mask, homemade polyester pants and top.
Mask manufactured by Collegeville Costumes, found in Chicago, Illinois.

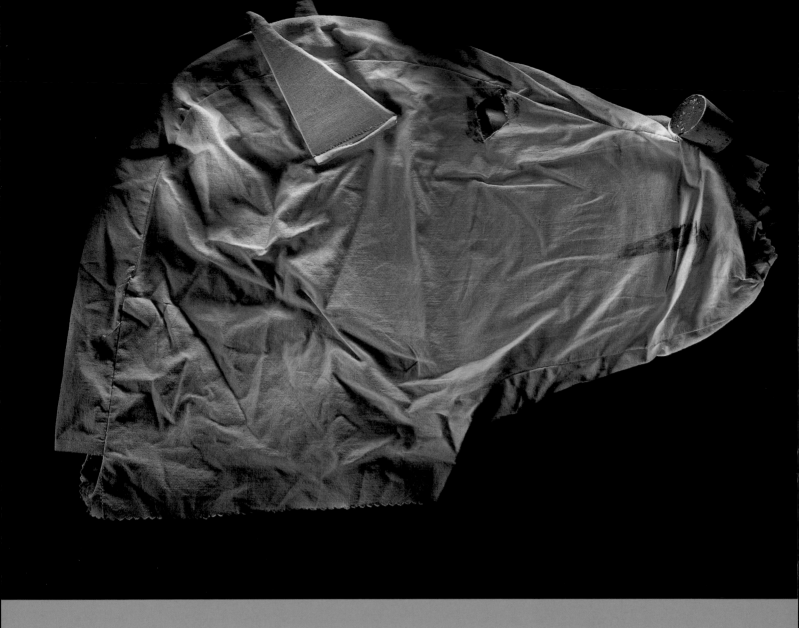

DOG MASK c. 1935–1940, cotton fabric stiffened with cardboard, cork nose. Homemade.

HUMPTY DUMPTY c. 1950, cotton jumpsuit with snaps up back, elastic wrists and ankles. Manufactured by Collegeville Costumes.

BRIDE c. 1950s, polyester dress with buttons up back and separate sleeves that match sheer yoke inset, paper doily-and-flowers bouquet. Manufactured by Funtime Play Suits, New York City, found in Wheeling, West Virginia.

ANGEL c. 1930, chiffon and tinsel-covered wire. Homemade, found in Pennsylvania.

WITH GLOW MASK

HALLOWEEN

COSTUME

MADE OF FLAME RETARDANT MATERIAL

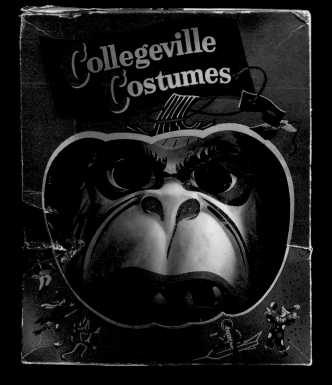

WITCH c. 1968, vinyl glow-in-the-dark mask, rayon costume with flocking. Manufactured by Collegeville Costumes.

MONSTER c. 1959, vinyl mask, rayon jumpsuit. Manufactured by Collegeville Costumes.

HALLOWEEN MASQUERADE SKELETON COSTUME c. 1956, plastic mask, rayon jumpsuit with printed skeleton. Manufacturer unknown.

TINKERBELL c. 1950s, painted buckram mask, rayon dress with "Tinkerbell" printed on chest. Manufactured by Bland Charnas Co.

UNCLE SAM c. late 1960s, rayon costume, plastic mask. Manufactured by Ben Cooper.

SECRET AGENT c. 1960s, vinyl "Chattermouth" mask, rayon-cotton costume. Manufactured by Ben Cooper, found in Toledo, Ohio.

FLOWER POWER GIRL c. 1970, rayon costume and wig, plastic mask. Manufactured by Collegeville Costumes, found in Salem, Massachusetts.

CLANCY THE ROBOT c. 1950s, plastic mask, rayon jumpsuit with silk-screened design. Manufactured by Ben Cooper

NASA ASTRONAUT c. early 1960s, plastic mask, rayon jumpsuit. Manufactured by Ben Cooper.

SPACE BUG c. 1959, plastic mask, rayon jumpsuit with glued-on glittery velveteen and paint.
Manufactured by Halco, found in Massachusetts.

GENIE MASK c. 1950s, vacuformed plastic. Manufacturer unknown.

FORTUNE TELLER dress, c. late 1920s–early 1930s, cotton top with drawstring at neck, cotton skirt with metal disks. Mask c. 1940s, waxed, painted buckram, Homemade.

BUDDIE BEATNIK c. 1960s, rayon costume, flocked plastic mask. Manufactured by Ben Cooper, found in Loveland, California.

WITCH DOCTOR c. 1952, cotton mask and silk-screened jumpsuit. Manufactured by Collegeville Costumes, found in Auburn, New York.

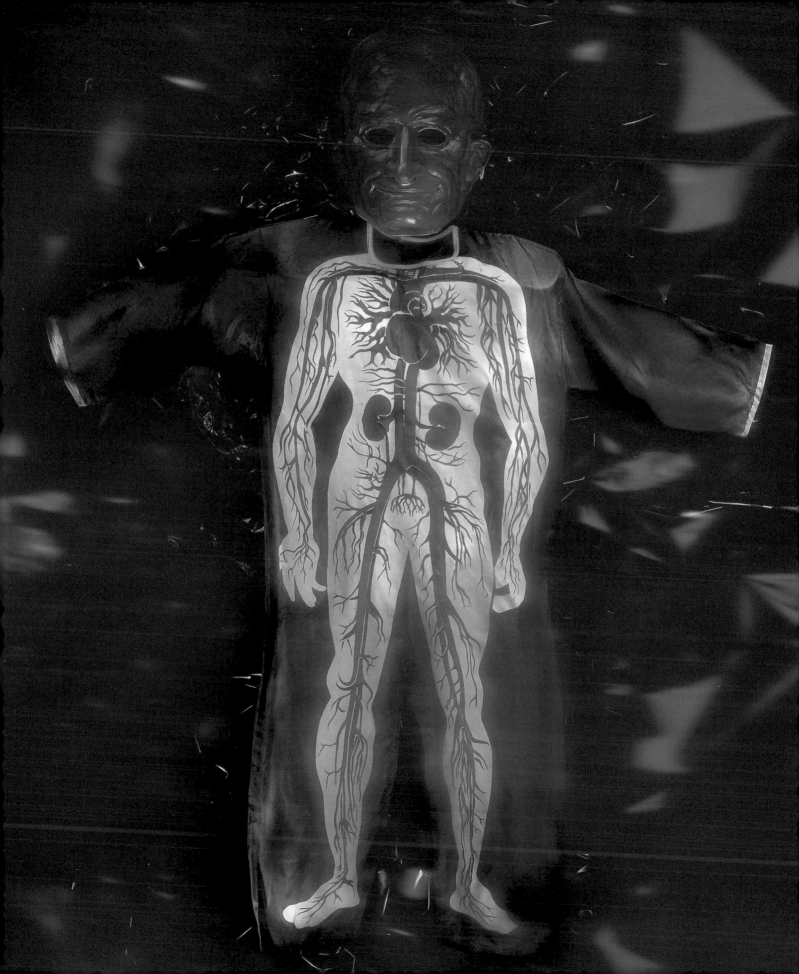

{RESOURCES}

books

APKARIAN-RUSSELL, PAMELA E. *The Tastes and Smells of Halloween: A Cookbook–Bogie Book.* Winchester, N.H.: Trick or Treat Trader Publications, 2001.

BANNATYNE, LESLEY PRATT. *Halloween: An American Holiday, an American History.* Gretna, La.: Pelican Publishing, 1990.

BLOOM, SOL. *George Washington Play and Pageant Costume Book.* Washington, D.C.: U.S. George Washington Bicentennial Commission, 1931.

CHIZMAR, RICHARD, AND ROBERT MORRISH, eds. *October Dreams: A Celebration of Halloween.* Abingdon, MD: Cemetery Dance Publications, 2000.

HOLLOWAY, JOSEPH E., AND WINIFRED K. VASS. *The African Heritage of American English.* Bloomington: Indiana University Press, 1993, 1997.

KUGELMASS, JACK. *Masked Culture: The Greenwich Village Halloween Parade.* New York: Columbia University Press, 1994.

LINTON, RALPH. *Halloween Through Twenty Centuries.* New York: Schuman, 1950.

MARKALE, JEAN. *The Pagan Mysteries of Halloween.* Rochester, Vt.: Inner Traditions International, 2001.

SANTINO, JACK, ed. *Halloween and Other Festivals of Death and Life.* Knoxville: University of Tennessee Press, 1994.

SCHNEIDER, STUART, AND BRUCE ZALKIN. *Halloween: Costumes and Other Treats.* Atglen, Pa.: Schiffer Books, 2001.

WORRELL, ESTELLE. *Children's Costume in America, 1607–1910.* New York: Scribner, 1980.

Masquerade and Carnival: Their Customs and Costumes. Paris and New York: Butterick Publishing Co., 1892, 1900.

miscellaneous

DENNISON BOGIE BOOKS AND PARTY MAGAZINES, Framingham, Mass.: Dennison Manufacturing Co., 1908–1931.

Fashion Theory: The Journal of Dress, Body, and Culture. Oxford and New York: Berg Publishers.

MASQUERADE COSTUMES. New York: Home Pattern Company for *Ladies Home Journal*, 1910–1930s.

PRINCESS MASKS (Queen of Hearts, left; Cinderella, right), c. 1961, plastic masks with elastic bands. Both masks manufactured by Collegeville Costumes.

{ACKNOWLEDGMENTS}

I am deeply indebted to Howard Reeves at Harry N. Abrams for taking on this project, along with Emily Farbman and Brankica Kovrlija. Their commitment to my work brought my project to life. A special thank-you to Eric Himmel for introducing me to Howard, and believing in me and supporting this project.

I would like to thank Mark Alice Durant for his illuminating essay, which helps to clarify and focus for the reader my visual imagination. I appreciate his patience throughout for the many demands I made in dealing with my obsessions.

My appreciation to Valerie Steele for providing a foreword for the book and for her enthusiasm throughout the project.

While handling my collection I became more appreciative of the men and women who worked in the costume-manufacturing industry. I would like to pay tribute to all the costume makers who at the turn of the century often hand-sewed part of the costumes, silk-screened designs, and individually painted the gauze masks, and who also often worked under difficult conditions.

During 1998–1999, I was granted a sabbatical from my position as photography professor at the University at Albany, State University of New York, that enabled me to focus on this project, and for that I am grateful. The Polaroid Studio in New York City and John Reuter and Barbara Hitchcock are especially thanked for their early support. The 4x5 view camera I used was provided by Sinar Bron Imaging thanks to William Andrews and Lee Edwards.

The assistance of my studio assistant, Ray Felix, has been invaluable, and he is due a large share of credit for the realization of this project. Ray assisted me with lighting, set building, and many other aspects of production. I am also indebted to photographer Mark McCarty for his many valuable contributions concerning lighting and other technical issues. Robert DeLuna often volunteered to help during photo shoots. And I thank him. Additional thanks to Richard Wager and Chris Costan, who painted wonderful backdrops that helped bring the costumes to life. Phillip Retzky, Norman Brosterman, Janet West, Sandra Winter, Martha Barnes, and Polly Dufresne assisted me in finding wonderful costumes.

Laura Reinhardt organized all my computer work, Dan Claro created a database, and Stephanie Klose captioned and identified many of the materials used in the costume tableaux and I am indeed grateful. Charles Duncan provided technical assistance scanning old fabrics and materials. Valerie Steele and Ellen Shanley, Curator of Costume, from the Fashion Institute of Technology, and Phyllis Magidson, Curator of Costumes and Textiles from the Museum of the City of New York, also helped to place the costumes in historical context, information which is most valuable to this book.

Friends Marijo Dougherty and Norman Bauman were supportive at each stage of production, even to driving two newborn lambs from upstate New York to Chelsea so Bo Peep could have her sheep.

Sam Cornish of Collegeville/Imagineering; David Bartolino of Spooky World, "America's Horror Theme Park;" Ira Cooper, son of Ben Cooper; and Pam Apkarian-Russell, known as the Halloween Queen, provided information on Halloween and the costume companies.

My mother, Rhoda, and family members Marsha, David, and Laurie Galembo and Deborah Birnbaum provided support throughout. As well, many old friends and a few new ones, especially Eva Sutton, Marcia Lippman, Joanne Lue, Roberta Bernstein, Chris Drago, David Formaneck, Danny Goodwin, Armando Moutela, Caroline Owerka, Shelly Rice, Bill Hunt, Allen Harris, Ronit Leora, Anne Petter, Trilbey Schreiber, Henry Drewal, Sarah Khan, Edwidge Danticat, C. Daniel Dawson, Mark Schreyer, Sandy Skolnick, Irving Solero, Anne Turyn, Lorraine Walsch, and Cheryl Younger were there for me whenever I needed assistance. Michelle Rubin of Writers House was extremely generous in providing input into the project.

I especially thank all the patient and cooperative children who served as models and transporters of magic to the costumes: Giovanni Alexandre, Peter Anderson, Quana Victorina Barrett, Nicole Beckford, Scott Behr, Arielle and Camille Blake, Brandy, Alessandra Brawn, Krystal Burgess, Crystal Inez Camacho, Hanna Carlson, Nikola Caruso, Adrian and Marie Castro, Jane Adrienne Charles-Voltaire, Anne Connelly, Camille and Isabella Costan-Toth, Cesar and Elizabeth Cruz, Megan Danielle Cruz, Asia de Jesus, Adah Dextrious, Pierce Carlton Doyle, Allegra and Alexandra Fasulo, Asia Fisher, Noah, Hailey, Chelsea, and Corey Galembo, Anna Hagen, Gus and Russell Jacobs, Syavash Jefferson, David Johnson, Keeana Kee, Eve Klein, Nina Kuo, Asher Lack, Julia, Emma, and Aidan Landauer, Joanna Landow, Alexander Leriche, Michelle Lopez, Olivia Mardwig, Kate McCarty, Haille and TeFarii McKenzie, Emily Miller, Omar Moid, Rachel Murphy, Sonrisa Murray-Fox, Anya Nordstrom, Joshua and Brianna Ocasio, Joy Ofili, Jacob Ramos, Angela Rizzi, Danielle and Nicole Rodriguez, Shaday Elisa Rodriguez, India Rogers-Shepp, Tanya Ruiz, Marina Samuels, Eve and Nell Sappol, Jesse and Preston Small, Salome Stulberg, Zane Tatro, Enola Celest Trotman, Ayane Tsutsumi, Kate Lynn Walsh, Graciela and Julian Watrous, Gabrielle Williams, and Blaise and Gus Yafcak.

Page 2: **BAT** c. 1920s, cotton fabric, rice paper teeth. Homemade, found in Indiana.

Page 3: **ELF** c. 1940s, painted buckram mask, polished cotton hat, rayon hair. Manufacturer unknown, found in North Carolina.

Pages 4-5: **LEOPARDS** c. 1950s, leopard-print flannel over buckram, with painted-on features and elastic bands. Manufactured by Ben Cooper.

Page 7: **HANDS** c. 1930s, waxed, painted buckram. Manufactured by Halco.

FEET c. 1930s, waxed, painted buckram soleless shoes. Manufactured by Halco.

editor Howard W. Reeves, with the assistance of Emily Farbman
designer Brankica Kovrlija
production manager Alyn Evans

LIBRARY OF CONGRESS CATALOGING-IN-PUBLICATION DATA
Galembo, Phyllis.
  Dressed for thrills : one hundred years of Halloween costume and masquerade / [photographs] by Phyllis Galembo ; essays by Mark Alice Durant ; foreword by Valerie Steele.
    p. cm.
Includes bibliographical references.
  ISBN 0-8109-3291-1
  1. Halloween costumes—History. 2. Halloween costumes—Pictorial works. I. Galembo, Phyllis. II. Title.
  GT4965 .D87 2002
  394.2646—dc21

                        2002003236

Printed and bound in Hong Kong
10 9 8 7 6 5 4 3 2 1

Harry N. Abrams, Inc.
100 Fifth Avenue
New York, N.Y. 10011
www.abramsbooks.com

Abrams is a subsidiary of
 LA MARTINIÈRE
GROUPE